ENGINEERING
DISASTERS

THE SPACE SHUTTLE *CHALLENGER*

BY TODD KORTEMEIER

CONTENT CONSULTANT
Robin Dillon-Merrill, PhD
Professor, McDonough School of Business
Georgetown University

Cover image: *Challenger* launches from Cape Canaveral, Florida, on January 28, 1986.

Core Library
An Imprint of Abdo Publishing
abdobooks.com

abdobooks.com

Published by Abdo Publishing, a division of ABDO, PO Box 398166, Minneapolis, Minnesota 55439.

Printed in the United States of America, North Mankato, Minnesota
102019
012020

THIS BOOK CONTAINS RECYCLED MATERIALS

Cover Photo: NASA
Interior Photos: NASA, 1, 4–5, 9, 12–13, 17, 26–27, 43, 45; Everett Collection/Newscom, 7, 22; AP Images, 11; Shutterstock Images, 15 (space shuttle); Alxey Pnferov/iStockphoto, 15 (background); Dennis Cook/AP Images, 20–21; Red Line Editorial, 28; Scott Stewart/AP Images, 30; John Duricka/AP Images, 34–35; Zuma Archive/ZumaPress/Newscom, 40

Editor: Marie Pearson
Series Designer: Ryan Gale

Library of Congress Control Number: 2019942038

Publisher's Cataloging-in-Publication Data

Names: Kortemeier, Todd, author.
Title: The space shuttle Challenger / by Todd Kortemeier
Description: Minneapolis, Minnesota : Abdo Publishing, 2020 | Series: Engineering disasters | Includes online resources and index.
Identifiers: ISBN 9781532190759 (lib. bdg.) | ISBN 9781532176609 (ebook)
Subjects: LCSH: Challenger (Spacecraft)--Accidents--Juvenile literature | Space shuttles--Juvenile literature. | Disasters--Juvenile literature. | Engineering--Juvenile literature. | Space travel--Juvenile literature.
Classification: DDC 363.12465--dc23

CONTENTS

CHAPTER
ONE

A CHILLY MORNING

By 1986, sending men and women into space felt routine. STS-51L was the twenty-fifth mission of the space shuttle program for the National Aeronautics and Space Administration (NASA). After the mission, the space shuttle could land like an airplane. It could then be used again and again.

But there was something different about STS-51L. Christa McAuliffe was on board. She was not an astronaut. She was a high school teacher from New Hampshire. She was going to be the first teacher to go into space.

Before STS-51L, Christa McAuliffe trained in a special aircraft that simulates weightlessness by flying in steep dives.

She was a part of NASA's Teacher in Space program. Students around the country were watching her make history.

The space shuttle used for STS-51L was *Challenger*. The mission was supposed to launch on the afternoon of January 22, 1986. But it got pushed back several times. First the previous shuttle mission took longer than expected. Then there was bad weather at one of the

PERSPECTIVES

FIRST TEACHER IN SPACE

As a girl, Christa McAuliffe had excitedly watched the Apollo space program in the 1960s. When she applied for the Teacher in Space program, she wrote, "I watched the Space Age being born and I would like to participate." McAuliffe was excited for her journey and the new way she was going to be able to educate students. It was a role she took very seriously. "I would like to humanize the space age by giving a perspective from a non-astronaut, because I think the students will look at that and say, 'This is an ordinary person. This ordinary person is contributing to history,'" she said.

Icicles hung from the launchpad the morning of the launch.

landing sites. Then there was bad weather at the launch site in Cape Canaveral, Florida. The launch was finally set for January 28. McAuliffe told her parents she was ready to go.

LIFTOFF

The weather that morning was very cold for Florida. The temperature was 36 degrees Fahrenheit (2°C). It was the coldest launch in shuttle history. But despite the weather, the shuttle was cleared to launch. *Challenger* lifted off at 11:38 a.m.

All was normal for the first minute. *Challenger*'s rocket engines propelled it into the sky at full power. At 59 seconds into the flight, a small flame appeared on the right Solid Rocket Booster. The space shuttle had two of these boosters, one on each side. They were attached to a large external tank (ET) that held propellant for *Challenger*'s main engines. The flame grew until it was spitting a stream of fire into the air.

As the flight continued, wind pushed the flame onto the external tank. But *Challenger* continued as normal. Mission control radioed *Challenger* to say, "Go with throttle up." That meant the ship's engines were at full power and working properly.

Challenger commander Dick Scobee radioed back to confirm. His ship was traveling at nearly 2,000 miles per hour (3,200 km/h). It was 70 seconds

Members of mission control tried to figure out what was wrong with the shuttle.

into the flight. "Roger, go with throttle up," Scobee said. His words were the last ones received from the shuttle.

In an instant, flames overwhelmed *Challenger* and its rockets. The vehicle burst into a fireball. The two boosters flew away uncontrolled. For a moment, nobody knew what had happened. But there was no doubt something had gone terribly wrong.

Mission control studied its instruments. It watched to see if *Challenger* had survived the explosion and could come back and land. But as the seconds went on, it was clear what had happened. *Challenger* and its crew of seven were gone.

"The vehicle has exploded," NASA announcer Steve Nesbitt said. "The flight director confirms that."

The crowd at Cape Canaveral, which included McAuliffe's parents, gasped in horror. Millions of students around the country looked on from their classrooms. A nightmare became reality.

CHALLENGER

Challenger was originally built to be a space shuttle test vehicle. But in 1979, it was turned into a shuttle that could be used for real missions. *Challenger* was named for an old British research ship. The ship had explored both the Pacific and Atlantic oceans in the late 1800s. *Challenger* was the second shuttle in the NASA fleet after *Columbia.* The *Challenger* flew its first mission on April 4, 1983. In its career, it made history as the first shuttle to launch and land at night. STS-51L was *Challenger*'s tenth and final flight.

At first, spectators didn't realize that the smoke meant an explosion.

Three minutes after launch, NASA declared a contingency. Nobody was allowed in or out because there was important work to do. All data was backed up and stored. That data would help determine what brought down the space shuttle *Challenger*.

The *Challenger* disaster shook public confidence in spaceflight. It forced NASA to look at every aspect of its safety policies. No American could be sent to space again until the problem was fixed.

CHAPTER TWO

THE SHUTTLE

On May 25, 1961, President John F. Kennedy gave NASA an ambitious goal. By the end of the decade, put a man on the moon and return him safely back to Earth. The Soviet Union's space program was working hard toward the same goal. But it was NASA that did what seemed impossible. On July 20, 1969, US astronaut Neil Armstrong stepped on the surface of the moon during the Apollo project.

NASA was in transition during the 1970s. The Apollo project involved many thousands of people and billions of dollars. NASA flew moon missions until 1972. By then, the costs were too much. Each Apollo spacecraft could only

Neil Armstrong photographed Edwin Aldrin on the moon.

be used once. The final moon landing was Apollo 17. NASA developed a new vehicle. NASA hoped to make space travel cheaper and more frequent.

MAKING SPACEFLIGHT MORE AFFORDABLE

The new vehicle was reusable. It was commonly called the space shuttle. Officially, it was the Space Transport System (STS). It had three main parts. These parts were the orbiter, the ET, and the boosters. The orbiter held the crew and the cargo. The orbiter was designed like an airplane. After the mission, it glided down to land on Earth. The orbiter had three main engines. The propellant for these engines was in the ET.

At the start of a mission, the main engines and boosters blasted the orbiter into the sky. After approximately two minutes, the boosters used up their propellant. They separated from the shuttle and fell back to Earth. The main engines kept working, pushing the shuttle the rest of the way to space. When the

THE SPACE SHUTTLE

This diagram identifies the orbiter, external tank, and Solid Rocket Boosters of a space shuttle. Why do you think the space shuttle needed two boosters? How does this diagram help you understand how the space shuttle worked?

ET was empty, the main engines shut down. The ET separated from the shuttle and fell to Earth. The orbiter was now in space.

Columbia was the first orbiter built. Its first mission was on April 12, 1981. *Challenger* was the second orbiter. It flew its first mission on April 4, 1983. *Challenger* made several historic flights. Guion S. Bluford became the first African American in space on August 30, 1983. Sally Ride became the first woman in space on June 18, 1983.

McAULIFFE'S BACKUP

Christa McAuliffe's backup was Barbara Morgan. Morgan was an elementary school teacher from Idaho. Even after the disaster, she still wanted to go into space. She continued to work with NASA's education division. And in 1998, she was chosen to enter the astronaut program. She flew in space aboard the shuttle *Endeavour* in 2007. She left NASA in 2008 and returned to education.

THE MISSION AND ITS CREW

The STS-51L mission was scheduled to orbit Earth for about a week.

The STS-51L crew posed for a photo. In the front row, *from left to right*, are Michael Smith, Dick Scobee, and Ronald McNair. In the back row are Ellison Onizuka, Christa McAuliffe, Gregory Jarvis, and Judith Resnik.

The astronauts would do some experiments. They would launch a satellite. Christa McAuliffe was going to record educational lessons. This was the second flight for four of the astronauts. Dick Scobee was the mission commander. He had already flown on *Challenger* in 1984. Ellison Onizuka, Judith Resnik, and Ronald McNair were all mission specialists. They would handle the nonflying duties. They would also do scientific experiments. All had previously flown. Resnik was the second woman in space. She flew on *Discovery* in 1984. Physicist McNair was the second African American in space. He flew on *Challenger* in 1984.

McAuliffe, pilot Michael Smith, and payload specialist Gregory Jarvis were all making their first spaceflights. Jarvis was the only astronaut besides McAuliffe who was not a government employee. He entered the astronaut program as an employee of Hughes Aircraft. Hughes made parts for NASA.

In five years of spaceflight, the shuttle experienced no accidents. NASA's last major accident had taken place in 1970. But no person had ever been lost after liftoff. That all changed with the *Challenger* disaster.

PERSPECTIVES

ELLISON S. ONIZUKA

Ellison S. Onizuka was born in Hawaii in 1946. He used to look up at the sky and dream of going into space. He became the first Japanese American astronaut in 1978. In 1985, he became the first Asian American to fly in space. "Your vision is not limited by what your eye can see, but by what your mind can imagine," he once said. "Make your life count—and the world will be a better place because you tried."

STRAIGHT TO THE SOURCE

Christa McAuliffe was a regular citizen. She spoke about the importance of regular people recording history in her application for the space program:

> *I want the students to also feel that they too are important, they too are participating in history. When I was thinking about doing a project for the space shuttle, I felt that doing a diary or a journal and keeping these notes would help personalize the space program. It would help other people connect with the space age. The students and the teachers and others who I would speak to would have somebody else's viewpoint, other than an astronaut's, to look through.*

Source: "Christa McAuliffe's Teacher in Space Interview." *TPT*. PBS, January 22, 2016. Web. Accessed August 1, 2019.

Changing Minds

McAuliffe states her belief that the experiences of regular people are important to the recording of history. Take a position on this viewpoint, then imagine that your best friend holds the opposite viewpoint. Write a short essay trying to change your friend's mind. Include facts and details to support your point.

CHAPTER THREE

PIECING THINGS TOGETHER

The *Challenger* disaster made headlines around the world. President Ronald Reagan was set to give his State of the Union address that night. But instead he addressed the nation with a tribute. The speech was considered one of the best presidential speeches in history. Near the end of the president's speech, he said, "We will never forget them, nor the last time we saw them, this morning, as they prepared for their journey and waved goodbye."

The *Challenger* recovery mission began immediately after the disaster.

President Ronald Reagan gave his speech about *Challenger* from the Oval Office in the White House.

Crews recover a piece of *Challenger* after the explosion.

Challenger exploded over the ocean at a height of 46,000 feet (14,000 m). The debris was spread out over an area seven times the size of Washington, DC.

It was the largest surface water search involving the US Coast Guard. It involved 14 ships and 11 airplanes. It cost NASA $1 million per week. The search and rescue team was able to pull some debris from the water. But most of the 3 million pounds (1.4 million kg) sank before it could be recovered.

Submarines carefully searched the seafloor. Any piece of the shuttle could be the key piece of evidence to what went wrong. Investigators wanted to recover every piece of *Challenger* possible. But there were a few priorities. The crew compartment and the boosters would be especially helpful in figuring out what happened.

FINDING THE CREW

The crew compartment was found in March. It was lying in only 100 feet (30 m) of water. Inside were the bodies of all seven crew members. The crew compartment was crushed from its impact with the water. Workers decided to haul the entire compartment to the surface. In the process, the body of Gregory Jarvis went missing.

THE *CHALLENGER* FLAG

One unusual piece of cargo carried on *Challenger* was an American flag. The flag was donated by a Boy Scout troop in Monument, Colorado. The flag survived the disaster. It was found still in its plastic bag. The flag was returned to Troop 514. It is now known as the *Challenger* Flag. The troop continues to display the flag. They take it to special events around Colorado for the public to see.

It took five weeks to find his body again. Astronauts Robert Crippen and Robert Overmyer were in charge of the recovery operation. At one point, Crippen used his personal credit card to hire a ship to search for Jarvis. His body was finally found again on April 15. Studying the crew cabin showed it was unlikely the astronauts died in the breakup of the shuttle. It is possible they survived until the crew cabin hit the water.

PERSPECTIVES

ROBERT OVERMYER

Robert Overmyer had flown *Challenger* himself. He knew the astronauts on STS-51L well. Overmyer volunteered his time to help search for the crew. He helped the investigation. It was unclear at first how long the crew survived. There was no question in Overmyer's mind as to how Scobee would have handled it. "I not only flew with Dick Scobee, we owned a plane together, and I know Scob did everything he could to save his crew. Scob fought for any and every edge to survive. He flew that ship without wings all the way down."

The boosters were found in April. A submarine located them in 600 feet (180 m) of water. By this time, signs pointed to the right booster as being the cause of the disaster. NASA officials would examine it.

Meanwhile, President Reagan appointed the Rogers Commission to investigate the disaster. The commission was named for its chairman, William P. Rogers. He was a former US secretary of state. The commission included politicians, scientists, and space experts. Astronauts Neil Armstrong and Sally Ride were both members. They worked to figure out what went wrong.

EXPLORE ONLINE

Chapter Three mentions Ronald Reagan's famous speech to the nation after the *Challenger* disaster. The website below contains the full speech. What new information did you learn by reading this speech?

REAGAN'S ADDRESS TO THE NATION

abdocorelibrary.com/space-shuttle-challenger

CHAPTER FOUR

FINDING THE CAUSE

It was hard for the public to get much information after the disaster. NASA was trying to figure out what happened. NASA officials would not answer most questions in the weeks after the disaster. Behind closed doors, NASA was focusing on the boosters. Review of close-up video footage showed a flame spouting from the right booster. This video was NASA's and not public. That led to false speculation in the news about the true cause of the crash. Finally, on February 13, NASA released pictures of the faulty booster.

Rogers Commission members William P. Rogers, *left*, and Sally Ride, *second from left*, examine a piece of a booster.

TIMELINE OF LAUNCH

Shuttle missions are timed throughout the duration of the spaceflight. "T" stands for time. Anything before the launch is "T-" and anything after is "T+." This is a timeline of Challenger's 73-second flight. How does this help you understand what happened?

T-06.000
Challenger's main engines start.

T=00.000
The boosters fire up, and *Challenger* lifts off.

T+00.678
The first plume of black smoke appears in *Challenger's* right booster.

T+03.375
Challenger is higher than the launchpad tower.

T+40.000
Challenger breaks the sound barrier at 767 miles per hour (1,234 km/h) and 19,000 feet (5,791 m) high.

T+58.788
A plume of flame begins to grow on the right booster, unnoticed by the crew or NASA.

T+60.004
Pressure in the right booster begins to drop, indicating a possible propellant leak.

T+66.764
Pressure begins to drop in the external tank, indicating the leak has spread there.

T+70.000
Commander Dick Scobee acknowledges a message from mission control, the last words received from the shuttle.

T+73.000
Pilot Michael Smith says, "Uh oh," over the crew intercom.

T+73.124
Challenger begins to disintegrate after the boosters and external tank start to destruct.

It was up to the Rogers Commission to find the answers. Its investigation lasted for months. The investigation included hearings, interviews, and research into any potential safety flaws.

The commission's final report was released June 9, 1986. Besides a problem with the booster, there was also a problem with NASA policies. The commission said there was sometimes disregard for safety.

THE O-RING DESIGN

A rubber seal called an O-ring had a crucial role on the space shuttle. Each booster had two O-rings at the three joints where the rocket was put together. These rings plugged the gaps so burning propellant could not escape.

The boosters were sealed in several places. The O-ring was flexible. If the rocket bent or twisted under the extreme force of liftoff, the O-ring could fill in a gap that might open. The O-ring was the last line of defense. If it failed, there was no stopping hot gases

Richard Feynman of the Rogers Commission explained the weaknesses of the O-ring to reporters.

from burning through. And at that point, it would be too late to save the mission. Engineers knew about this risk when designing the shuttle in 1971.

Shuttle boosters were manufactured by a company called Morton Thiokol Incorporated (MTI). MTI and NASA both knew that there could be problems with the O-rings. Early tests showed that metal could bend and widen the gap around the rings. Early shuttle missions showed evidence of this. But MTI and NASA decided not to fix the problem. They treated it as a risk of spaceflight. The commission concluded this was one factor that led to the disaster.

THE DECISION TO LAUNCH

Cold weather was another way to damage the O-ring. After being in cold temperatures, the rubber O-ring did not spring back right away. It took some

PERSPECTIVES

ROGER BOISJOLY

Six months before the *Challenger* disaster, MTI engineer Roger Boisjoly predicted O-ring failure to his managers. When it came time to launch *Challenger*, Boisjoly protested. He and three other MTI engineers tried to stop the launch. When it went ahead, Boisjoly thought *Challenger* would explode on the launchpad. When it lifted off successfully, he thought the danger was over. "And when we were one minute into the launch a friend turned to me and said, 'Oh God. We made it. We made it!'" Boisjoly said. "Then, a few seconds later, the shuttle blew up. And we all knew exactly what happened."

time to regain its shape. That meant it could not fill a gap quickly.

Challenger launched in record-low temperatures. It was 36 degrees Fahrenheit (2°C) that morning. The previous coldest launch was at 53 degrees (12°C). Even at that warmer temperature, a gap had opened between the O-ring and the booster. But in that case, the flight continued safely.

Several people were concerned about the *Challenger* launching in cold temperatures. They knew that the cold could mean disaster. MTI engineer Bob Ebeling had warned about it in 1985.

FEYNMAN'S DEMONSTRATION

Richard Feynman was a scientist on the Rogers Commission. After the disaster, he demonstrated the effect of cold on a rubber O-ring. He did so in a televised hearing. He took a sample of the rubber and bent it with a clamp. He then placed it in a glass of ice water. When he took the rubber out, it held its bent shape. It didn't go back to a circle.

When NASA saw the weather forecast, it remembered the warning and called MTI on January 27.

MTI said not to launch. But NASA needed to know more. What was the risk? And what would be a safe temperature to launch? MTI quickly prepared a presentation. NASA was faced with a very difficult decision. The launch had already been delayed many times. It was not easy to make a decision like this on short notice. But NASA wanted to launch. And MTI did not want to disagree with its customer. Two of three MTI managers voted to launch. With that guidance, NASA gave the go-ahead.

FURTHER EVIDENCE

Chapter Four discusses the causes of the *Challenger* disaster. What was one of the main points of the chapter? What evidence is used to support this point? Read the article at the website below. Does the information from the website support the main point of the chapter? Does it present new evidence?

CHALLENGER EXPLOSION

abdocorelibrary.com/space-shuttle-challenger

CHAPTER FIVE

RETURN TO FLIGHT

The Rogers Commission identified all that went wrong in the *Challenger* disaster. It made several recommendations on how to fix the problems. The boosters had to be redesigned. The joints were strengthened to keep the O-ring seal tighter. A third O-ring was added for extra safety. MTI was made to fix the boosters at its own expense. It was also fined $10 million. But MTI accepted no legal responsibility for the accident.

NASA also had to change its internal structure. It created a new department to oversee safety. And the launch schedule was

Roger Boisjoly, an engineer for MTI, spoke about his reservations on launching in cold temperatures in June 1986.

spaced out. Workers at NASA often felt rushed by all the launches NASA wanted. Giving them more time meant more time for safety. And more astronauts were placed into management positions. Nobody knew what astronauts needed like other astronauts.

MAKING CHANGES

The report was damaging to NASA. NASA had to take steps to fix its problems. The Rogers Commission kept an eye on the work. There was never going to be zero risk in spaceflight. And it was easy to say what should have been done differently after the fact. But by 1988, NASA felt it had done all it could do to

REMEMBERING THE ASTRONAUTS

The remains of all seven astronauts were flown to Dover Air Force Base in Delaware. A small ceremony was held there before the remains were released to their families. Some astronauts, including McAuliffe, were buried near their homes. Some were buried at Arlington National Cemetery. There is also a marker there dedicated to the crew's memory.

reduce the risk. The space shuttle *Discovery* was set to launch in September.

STS-26 launched on September 29. It had been 32 months since the disaster. Only a few changes were noticeable to the crew. The *Challenger* crew had worn simple space suits. The suits had no pressurized oxygen to keep them alive if they had to escape. Going forward, all crew members had to wear pressure suits during launch and landing. The *Discovery* mission went off with no issues.

COLUMBIA

NASA's many changes began a long period of safe spaceflight. Among the shuttle's major achievements was launching the Hubble Space Telescope. The telescope let scientists see distant objects and learn more about the universe.

But that period of success ended in 2003. The shuttle *Columbia* was destroyed upon reentry. All seven astronauts were killed. The disaster reminded many of what had happened to *Challenger* 17 years earlier.

Columbia was doomed from launch. A piece of insulating foam fell from the external tank and struck the orbiter's wing on liftoff. NASA noticed this after reviewing video of the launch. They feared the impact opened a hole in the shuttle's heat shield. Reentering Earth's atmosphere creates a lot of heat. Without an intact heat shield, the shuttle

PERSPECTIVES

COLUMBIA ACCIDENT INVESTIGATION

The investigation into the *Columbia* disaster had conclusions similar to those from the *Challenger* investigation. NASA's decision-making sometimes came up short where safety was concerned. But investigators also recognized spaceflight always had risks. Investigators said that risk shouldn't prevent further exploration. The final report said, "(Spaceflight) involves a substantial element of risk, which must be recognized, but never accepted with resignation. The seven *Columbia* astronauts believed that the risk was worth the reward."

could burn up. But the shuttle was in orbit. It was too late to do anything. NASA's worst fears were confirmed when *Columbia* burned up on its return.

An investigation again found lapses in NASA safety. The foam problem had been seen before. But NASA had chosen to do nothing about it. NASA had to make changes again. The shuttle program was put on hold.

END OF AN ERA

The shuttle was grounded for 30 months. Most missions after were flown only to the International Space Station (ISS). If there was a problem on launch like *Columbia* had, the crew could stay on the ISS and wait for rescue.

After 30 years, the space shuttle program ended in 2011. Rising costs and different spaceflight priorities were major factors. NASA moved on to developing new rockets and spacecraft. It looked ahead to a future mission to Mars.

The Space Shuttle *Challenger* Memorial in Arlington National Cemetery preserves the memory of the *Challenger*'s crew.

The shuttle made reusable spacecraft possible. It accomplished many things. NASA was not giving up on spaceflight or exploration. But it needed to do so in a safe environment. Still, spaceflight will always carry some risk. People who become astronauts accept this risk. Today's daring astronauts continue going into space.

STRAIGHT TO THE **SOURCE**

In a high-pressure situation, it can be hard to make a decision, as noted by statistics expert Edward Tufte:

> *For* Challenger, *there were substantial pressures to get it off the ground as soon as possible: an unrealistic and over-optimistic flight schedule based on the premise that launches were a matter of routine . . . the difficulty for the rocket-maker (Morton-Thiokol) to deny the demands of its major client (NASA); and a preoccupation with public relations and media events. . . . But these pressures would not have prevailed over credible evidence against the launch, for many other flights had been delayed in the past for good reasons.*

Source: Edward Tufte. *Visual Explanations*. Cheshire, CT: Gravity Press, 1997. p 30. Web. *Wisconsin Space Grant Consortium*. Accessed August 2, 2019.

Consider Your Audience

Review this passage. Consider how you would adapt it for a different audience, such as your younger friends. Write a blog post conveying this same information for the new audience. How does your new approach differ from the original text, and why?

FAST FACTS

- STS-51L was a space shuttle mission flown by *Challenger* that launched January 28, 1986.
- The mission was notable for carrying Christa McAuliffe, who was to become the first teacher in space.
- Approximately 73 seconds into the mission, *Challenger* was destroyed, killing all seven crew members.
- The Rogers Commission investigated the accident and determined its cause.
- The mechanical cause was the failure of a rubber O-ring that allowed gases to escape one of the shuttle's Solid Rocket Boosters and ignite its external tank, which caused the shuttle to disintegrate in a ball of flame.
- The other main factor was a lack of safety oversight and poor decisions made by NASA and the manufacturer of the rockets, Morton Thiokol Incorporated.
- The shuttle was grounded for 32 months while the Solid Rocket Booster was redesigned and new safety protocols were put into place.
- Though the changes made spaceflight safer, there still were improvements to be made, as seen by the destruction of the shuttle *Columbia* on reentry in 2003.

STOP AND THINK

Tell the Tale

Chapter Four describes the Rogers Commission's investigation into the *Challenger* disaster. Imagine you are one of the investigators. What questions would you want answered? Where would you start your investigation? Write 200 words about your plans.

Surprise Me

Chapter Four describes the causes of the *Challenger* disaster. After reading this chapter, what facts about the disaster surprised you the most? Write a few sentences about each fact. Why did you find these facts surprising?

You Are There

This book discusses spaceflight. Imagine you have been selected for a space mission. Write a letter home to your family about the experience of launching on a rocket and being in space. What things would you want to do in space? Be sure to add plenty of detail to your notes.

Another View

This book talks about who was to blame for the *Challenger* disaster. As you know, every source is different. Ask a librarian or another adult to help you find another source about this event. Write a short essay comparing and contrasting the new source's point of view with that of this book's author. What is the point of view of each author? How are they similar and why? How are they different and why?

GLOSSARY

booster
the part of a rocket that causes it to lift off the launchpad and begin its flight

debris
pieces broken off of a larger object

launchpad
the area where a spacecraft takes off from

mission control
both a group of people and the place where they gather to monitor a space mission from launch to landing

orbit
the path one object takes around a larger object in space

orbiter
the part of the space shuttle system that contains the crew and all its equipment

payload
items brought into space by a spacecraft

propellant
the fuel and other substances that make a rocket lift off

reentry
the process in which the shuttle comes down from space and through Earth's atmosphere to land

satellite
an object that orbits around a larger object in space

ONLINE RESOURCES

To learn more about the space shuttle *Challenger*, visit our free resource websites below.

Core Library CONNECTION
FREE! COMMON CORE MULTIMEDIA RESOURCES

Visit **abdocorelibrary.com** or scan this QR code for free Common Core resources for teachers and students, including vetted activities, multimedia, and booklinks, for deeper subject comprehension.

Booklinks NONFICTION NETWORK
FREE! ONLINE NONFICTION RESOURCES

Visit **abdobooklinks.com** or scan this QR code for free additional online weblinks for further learning. These links are routinely monitored and updated to provide the most current information available.

LEARN MORE

Doudna, Kelly. *Space Exploration*. Minneapolis, MN: Abdo Publishing, 2017.

Hamilton, S. L. *Astronaut*. Minneapolis, MN: Abdo Publishing, 2016.

INDEX

About the Author

Todd Kortemeier is a children's book author, sportswriter, and aviation enthusiast from Minneapolis.